CLOSE UP

SHARKS

D0379784

Created by Q2AMedia

www.q2amedia.com

Copyright © Leopard Learning 2009
www.leopardlearning.com

Editor Bill Becker
Publishing Director Chester Fisher
Client Service Manager Santosh Vasudevan
Project Manager Shekhar Kapur
Art Director Sumit Charles
Designers Prashant Kumar & Neha Kaul
Art Editor Sujatha Menon

10 9 8 7 6 5 4 3 2 1

ISBN: 978-81-905723-3-0

Printed in China

Picture Credits

t=top b=bottom l=left r=right m=middle bg=background

Cover Image: cbpix: Shutterstock.

Half Title: Denis Scott: Corbis.

Content Images: Rui Manuel Teles Gomes: Shutterstock.
Bg Rich Carey: Shutterstock.

4-5 Richard Herrmann: Photolibrary. **4-5**bg WebStudio24h: Shutterstock. **5**b Perrine Doug: Photolibrary. **6** SeaPics. **7** Earthtojames. **8-9** User: Zac Wolf: Wikimedia. **9** SeaPics. **10** JuniperCreek: Istockphoto. **11** SeaPics. **12** Robinson Ed: Photolibrary. **12-13**bg cbpix: Shutterstock. **13** SeaPics. **14** SeaPics. **14-15** SeaPics. **14-15**bg cbpix: Shutterstock. **16-17** Q2A Imagebank. **18-19** Jim Watt: Photolibrary. **19** Jeff Rotman: GettyImages. **20** Jeff Rotman: Nature Picture Library. **21** SeaPics. **22** Andre Maritz: Shutterstock. **22-23**bg Pinosub: Shutterstock. **23** Lingbeek: Istockphoto. **24** Nildo Scoop: Shutterstock.

Contents

What is a Shark?

Sharks are fish. They breathe through **gills**. They swim. They have fins.

Sharks are **unique**, too. Their bones are soft. Nearly all fish have **predators**. Sharks do not.

Dorsal fin

Gills

The huge great white shark weighs about 7,000 pounds.

Some sharks are huge.
Others are smaller than you!
Sharks come in different
colors and shapes. Some
have spots all over
their skin. Other
sharks have odd-
shaped heads.

Caudal
fin

Let's take a close-up
look at sharks.

This is a hammerhead shark.
It has better vision than most
other sharks.

Where do Sharks Live?

Sharks live in every ocean in the world. Almost all sharks live in **salt water**.

Remember there are hundreds of different sharks. Scientists think that about six different kinds of sharks live in **fresh water**.

The Greenland shark is also called the sleeper shark.

People think of sharks near warm beaches in the summer. Did you know that some sharks live in the cold? Greenland sharks like living in the very cold water of the Arctic Ocean.

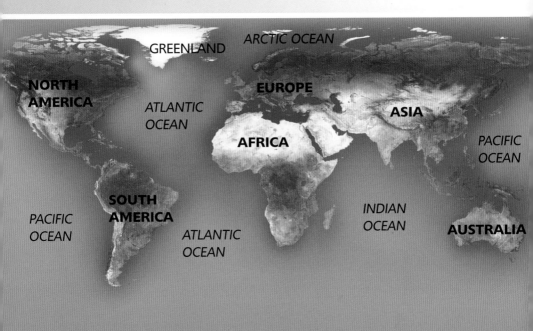

Find each ocean on the map. Sharks live in every one of them!

FACT

Some sharks can visit fresh water, but they cannot live there. They swim back to the ocean where the water is salty.

Shark Families

Some sharks stay in groups. Other sharks live most of their lives alone. A great white shark likes to swim and hunt alone.

When another shark swims too close, the great white will bite the shark. This is the way it says, "Back off!"

Other sharks spend almost all of their time in groups. Scalloped hammerheads and nurse sharks are **social** sharks.

Whale sharks spend most of their time alone.

Nurse sharks travel and hunt together.

Mothers and **Babies**

Almost all fish lay eggs. Sharks are fish, but only some of them lay eggs. Others have eggs that stay inside the mother's body. The baby shark hatches in its mother. The baby shark eats other eggs that have not hatched.

This is the egg of a cat shark.

Some sharks **bear** live young.
This means that the baby grows
inside the mother, but not in an
egg. The mother's body feeds the
baby. Your mother fed you
before you were born.

Lemon sharks
give birth to
live young.

Growing Up

Baby sharks are called pups. Mother sharks do not raise their babies. The pups must **defend** and hunt for themselves.

Shark pups take up to 15 years to become adults. Pups survive if bigger sharks or other creatures do not attack them while they are small.

This pup is small compared to the diver.

Sharks that live in groups have some **protection** from the other sharks. Sharks that live alone depend completely on themselves.

These hammerhead pups have a lot of growing to do!

How Sharks Eat

All sharks are predators. This means they prey on other animals, not plants. Each shark's mouth is made for the type of animal it eats.

With all these teeth, a shark's bite can do a lot of damage!

FACT

Sharks are always producing teeth. Some sharks make thousands of teeth in their lives.

Some sharks eat tiny animals, like **plankton**. Such sharks do not need teeth to bite or chew lankton.

Others sharks eat large animals, such as whales, dolphins, and other sharks. Sharks that eat big animals need sharp, strong teeth.

This basking shark filters plankton from the water.

No Sleep!

Have you ever owned a fish tank? You may have noticed that fish do not sleep as people do. Fish must rest in other ways.

Different sharks rest in different ways. Some stay still and rest. Their bodies draw water into their gills. This way the sharks can breathe but rest their bodies.

The great white shark cannot pull water into its gills. It must keep moving to breathe.

Other sharks must swim constantly. If they stop swimming, water will not flow through their gills. They cannot breathe. These sharks do not rest at all!

Gills take water into the shark's body like you breathe air through your mouth.

Shark Senses

Your senses help you move around and stay safe. Sharks use their senses, too.

Sharks have great distance vision. This helps them find **prey** when they hunt. Sharks have a great sense of smell, too.

The shark's nasal barbels feel things close to its mouth.

Sharks have a sense of touch like most animals do.

Sharks have an ear on each side of their heads. The ears are inside their heads instead of outside. They hear very well. Sharks even hear **vibrations** like splashing and swimming.

The shark's eyelid does not close completely.

FACT

Sharks taste, but not like you do. Their taste buds are on the sides of the mouth and tongue.

Shark Attacks

This is what a surfer looks like from underwater. To a shark, it looks like a turtle or a seal!

When a shark attacks a human, it makes the news. How much of a threat are sharks to humans?

There are hundreds of kinds of sharks. Only about 30 have ever bitten humans. Every year, sharks attack only about 70 people in the entire world.

shark's bite. You are more likely to be attacked by an alligator or struck by lightning.

Sharks do not want to eat people. Humans are too bony and hard to digest. Most shark attacks happen when the shark mistakes the human for another animal.

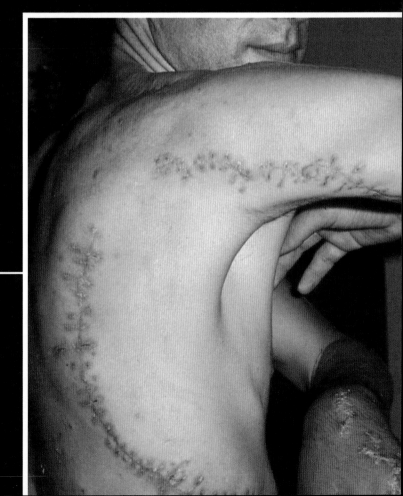

This man survived a shark bite.

Amazing
Shark Facts

What is a mermaid's purse?
A mermaid's purse is the name of the
shell of a shark's egg. (Look for one
on page 10.)

Can sharks chew?
No, they swallow their food in
big chunks.

Do sharks have any enemies?
Yes! Killer whales attack small
sharks. Some sharks attack
other sharks. Humans are
the greatest killer of sharks.

How long have sharks been on Earth?

Sharks have been on Earth for over 400 million years.

Are rays the same as sharks?

No, they are different animals but they are related.

What do the dents near the shark's mouth do?

They sense electricity from other animals.

Glossary

bear give birth to

defend to repel danger or an attack

fresh water water such as in lakes and rivers that is not salty

gills the part of a fish's body that takes oxygen from the water

plankton a very small swimming animal

predator an animal that hunts other animals

prey an animal that is hunted by another

protection the act of keeping something safe

salt water water such as in seas and oceans that is salty

social living in groups or communities

unique different or unusual

vibration a fast, trembling motion

Index